NORTHERN LIGHTS

David Whitfield

www.av2books.com

AV² provides enriched content that supplements and complements this book. Weigl's AV² books strive to create inspired learning and engage young minds in a total learning experience.

Your AV² Media Enhanced books come alive with...

Audio
Listen to sections of the book read aloud.

Key Words
Study vocabulary, and complete a matching word activity.

Video
Watch informative video clips.

Quizzes
Test your knowledge.

Embedded Weblinks
Gain additional information for research.

Slide Show
View images and captions, and prepare a presentation.

Try This!
Complete activities and hands-on experiments.

... and much, much more!

Go to **www.av2books.com**, and enter this book's unique code.

BOOK CODE

P 9 8 7 8 7 9

AV² by Weigl brings you media enhanced books that support active learning.

Published by AV² by Weigl
350 5ᵗʰ Avenue, 59ᵗʰ Floor
New York, NY 10118
Website: www.av2books.com   www.weigl.com

Library of Congress Control Number: 2012941686
ISBN 978-1-61913-098-2 (hard cover)
ISBN 978-1-61913-545-1 (soft cover)

Printed in the United States of America in North Mankato, Minnesota
1 2 3 4 5 6 7 8 9 16 15 14 13 12

062012
WEP170512

Editor Aaron Carr
Design Ken Clarke

Every reasonable effort has been made to trace ownership and to obtain permission to reprint copyright material. The publishers would be pleased to have any errors or omissions brought to their attention so that they may be corrected in subsequent printings.

Weigl acknowledges Getty Images as its primary image supplier for this title. Page 13, middle: courtesy of Packa.

CONTENTS

Auroras are produced by energy from the Sun colliding with Earth's **atmosphere**. However, the Sun does not always produce the same amount of energy. Sometimes, there are storms on the surface of the Sun that produce a great deal of energy. Auroras produced at these times are larger and brighter than auroras produced at other times. These auroras can also be seen from a far distance from Earth's poles.

Studying Northern Lights

High up in a cold, dark sky, nature puts on a dazzling show of shifting light. Green lights appear. They move around in the sky and are joined by flashes of yellow, red, pink, blue, or purple. These are the northern lights. Their scientific name is aurora borealis. Northern lights are usually seen during the winter months. They occur in northern **polar regions** on Earth.

Auroras also occur near Earth's south pole. These are known as aurora australis, or the southern lights. Since fewer people live near the south pole, these lights are seen less often, but they are no less colorful.

■ Auroras appear in pairs. When the aurora borealis is visible in the north, the aurora australis is also visible in the south.

How Northern Lights Form

The northern lights occur in the **thermosphere** high above Earth. The atmosphere contains many gases. The main gases in the atmosphere are oxygen and nitrogen. Northern lights occur when energy-charged **particles** from space strike the gases. The colliding particles cause the gases to glow different colors.

■ Auroras can appear up to 155 miles (250 kilometers) above Earth's surface.

NORTHERN LIGHTS MYTHS

Northern lights seemed magical to people long ago. They did not know what the lights were, so they created **myths** and legends about them. People in different parts of the world had their own stories about these colorful lights in the sky.

In Asia, some people thought northern lights were caused by dragons fighting in the sky. A legend belonging to the Menominee Indians in the United States tells that northern lights were giant torches used by friendly giants to help spear fish at night. In Finland, northern lights are called "fox fires." People thought the lights were made by an Arctic fox starting fires or scattering snow with its bushy tail.

Auroras and the Sun

Northern lights are created by the Sun. The Sun is the star closest to Earth. It is 93 million miles (150 million km) from Earth. The Sun controls Earth's weather and **climate**. It is so big Earth could fit inside it one million times. The Sun is a huge ball of fiery gases.

Storms on the surface of the Sun are called sunspots. During these storms, explosions called solar flares shoot energy-charged particles far out into space. It is these particles that create northern lights when they enter Earth's atmosphere.

■ Solar flares can reach temperatures of 36 million degrees Fahrenheit (20 million degree Celsius).

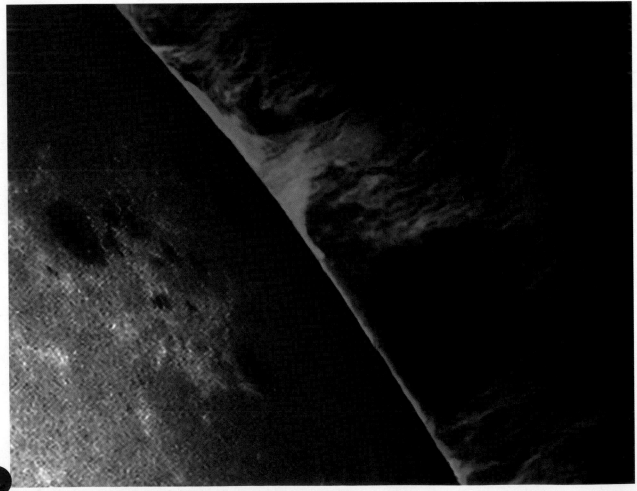

Solar Wind

Particles shot into space from the Sun are carried away by **solar winds**. These winds travel 200 to 500 miles (320 to 800 km) per second.

Billions of particles are carried in the solar wind. Some of them travel to Earth. It takes two to three days for the particles to travel through space to Earth. Some of these particles also travel to other planets. In fact, auroras occur on all planets in Earth's **solar system**.

The NASA spacecraft *Mariner 2* first tracked these particles coming from the Sun in 1962. It measured the solar wind while on a flight to Venus that lasted three and a half months.

■ In 2010, an aurora was spotted on Venus. This aurora measured about 2,100 miles (3,400 km) wide.

Magnetic Fields

Earth is like a giant magnet with ends, or poles, that pull toward each other. This attraction forms an invisible **magnetic field** around Earth. The field exists at every point on Earth's surface. Magnetic field lines help people visualize the direction of this field between the poles. The magnetic field is strongest near the north and south magnetic poles.

Some of the energy-charged particles in the solar wind are trapped by Earth's magnetic field. They are then drawn toward the poles.

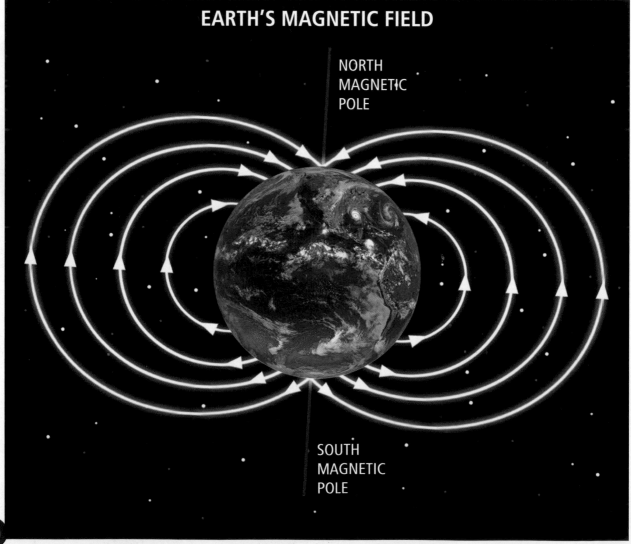

EARTH'S MAGNETIC FIELD

NORTH MAGNETIC POLE

SOUTH MAGNETIC POLE

THE AURORAL OVAL

As particles from the Sun enter Earth's atmosphere, they are guided into beams by the planet's magnetic field. The particles gather around the north and south magnetic poles in the shape of an oval.

In these ovals, particles strike gases in the atmosphere, causing them to glow as northern lights. Auroral ovals range in size from 60 to 620 miles (100 to 1,000 km) above the poles. From high above Earth, northern lights look like a giant glowing ring around the top of the planet.

Observing the Sun and Auroras

Observing the Sun

People can learn a great deal by studying the northern lights themselves, but they must also study the Sun for a full understanding of auroras. This is because the northern lights are produced by the action of the Sun. Scientists often use special equipment to study the Sun and the auroras it creates.

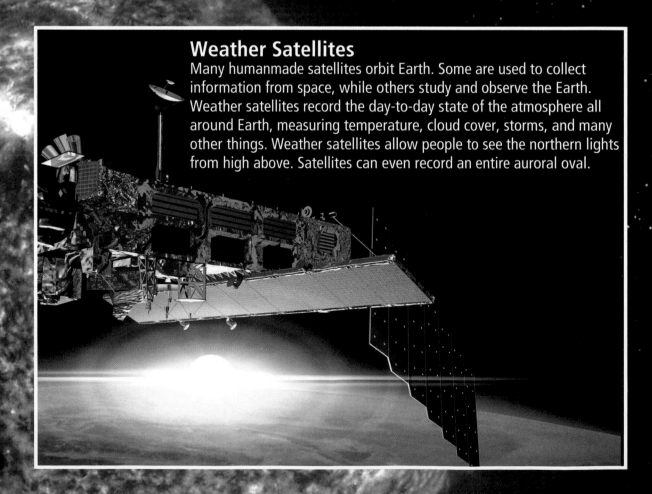

Weather Satellites

Many humanmade satellites orbit Earth. Some are used to collect information from space, while others study and observe the Earth. Weather satellites record the day-to-day state of the atmosphere all around Earth, measuring temperature, cloud cover, storms, and many other things. Weather satellites allow people to see the northern lights from high above. Satellites can even record an entire auroral oval.

Solar Observatories

Scientists can observe the Sun directly with powerful light-based telescopes. One of the largest of these is the McMath-Pierce Solar Telescope located at Kitt Peak in Arizona. Telescopes such as the McMath-Pierce provide important information about activity on the Sun that can affect the amount of solar wind that Earth receives.

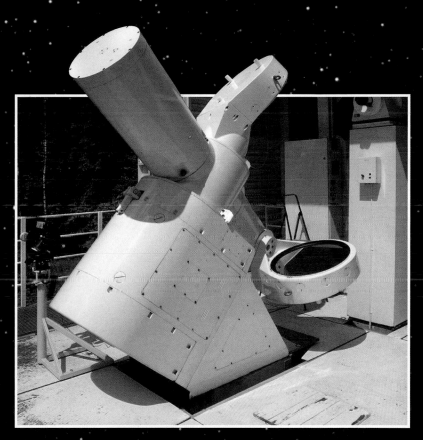

Spectrographs

Spectrographs are tools scientists use to measure light. A spectrograph divides light into the separate colors that make it up. These colors tell scientists what kinds of materials produced the light. This is how people discovered what sorts of gases make up the Sun, and what parts of the atmosphere glow to create auroras.

WHAT HAVE YOU LEARNED ABOUT STUDYING THE SKY?

These pages show some of the technology people use to study auroras. Use this book, and research in the library and online, to answer these questions.

1. Is there an observatory near where you live? What is it called?
2. Why are many observatories located at high **altitudes**?

Gases in the Atmosphere

Earth's atmosphere is made up of 78 percent nitrogen, 21 percent oxygen, and 1 percent other gases, such as hydrogen and helium. As the particles riding the solar wind enter Earth's atmosphere, they collide with these gases. The collisions cause the particles to release energy. This energy causes the gases to glow. The glowing lights are called auroras.

■ Green is the color most often seen in Earth's auroras.

AURORA COLORS

Most northern lights are shades of green. However, the color of northern lights depends on which gas is glowing. It also depends on how high above Earth the gas is located. Some gases, such as oxygen, occur at various altitudes. Oxygen below 155 miles (250 km) glows yellowish-green. Oxygen above this height glows red.

Hydrogen and Helium
blue and purple

Oxygen
red

155 miles (250 km)

Oxygen
yellowish-green

60 miles (100 km)

Nitrogen
blue and red

Viewing Auroras

People who live in the far north have the best view of the northern lights. Auroras are often in the night sky in this part of the world. During a period of large sunspots and solar flares, people living farther south may also see northern lights.

Fall, winter, and early spring are the seasons to watch for northern lights. The best time to see the lights is near midnight on a night when there is no moon and the sky is clear. However, northern lights can occur at any time of night.

■ The aurora borealis is most visible near the Arctic, but it has been seen from as far south as the United States.

Earth is not the only planet that has auroras. These lights can be seen on every planet throughout the solar system. Auroras on Jupiter's north and south poles are larger than Earth itself. Some of Jupiter's auroras are caused by solar winds and Jupiter's magnetic field, similar to how they are produced on Earth. Auroras on Jupiter are also produced by the magnetic fields of some of its moons. Venus has no magnetic field. On Venus, auroras are produced by solar wind alone, and are shaped differently than those on Earth.

Viewing the Northern Lights

Northern lights do not always appear the same. They occur in different shapes.

CURVED ARCS

Curved arcs can be hundreds of miles long. They look like trails through the sky.

AURORAL ARCS

Auroral arcs look like a shining curtain across the sky.

RAYED BANDS

When arcs are broken up into lines, they are known as rayed bands. These are often brighter and more colorful than arcs.

CORONAS

A corona looks like an explosion of light, with rays going in all directions from a central point.

Predicting Auroras

Particles from the Sun carried by solar winds are the main energy source for northern lights. In order to predict when northern lights will occur, scientists study the sunspots and solar flares that produce solar winds. When the solar wind is calm, there are few northern lights. When the wind is strong, Earth may have intense northern lights. As solar winds approach Earth, they pass a satellite. This satellite "reads" the winds and alerts scientists when auroras are likely to occur.

■ Scientists use satellites to predict when auroras will occur.

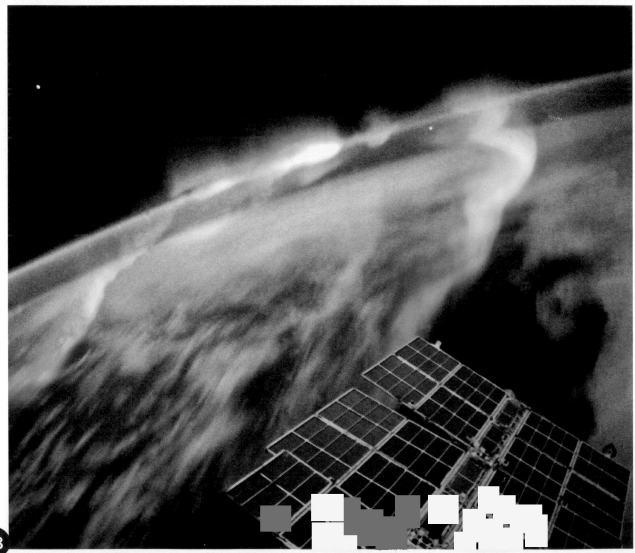

What is a Physicist?

A physicist is a scientist who studies the physical forces at work in the universe. Physicists study heat, light, magnetism, motion, and other forces. They use mathematics to describe these forces, and to predict how they will interact with one another.

Not everything that physicists study is easy to observe. The inside of a star, such as the Sun, or places far from Earth's surface often cannot be measured directly. Physicists must often use large and powerful machines called particle accelerators to reproduce these conditions, where forces behave in ways that are not seen on Earth. By using these machines, physicists can learn about events such as solar flares and auroras, and even about the beginnings of the universe.

Kristian Birkeland

Kristian Birkeland was a Norwegian scientist and explorer. In 1896, he was the first person to create auroras in a laboratory. Birkeland predicted that northern lights were caused by particles from the Sun being captured in Earth's magnetic field. These particles moved along the field into regions around the north and south poles. Birkeland's image was added to the 200 Norwegian **kroner** in 1994 in recognition of his achievements.

■ The CERN Large Hadron Collider near Geneva, Switzerland, is the largest particle accelerator in the world.

Eight Facts About the Northern Lights

Northern lights can be seen from space. Scientists use satellites and spacecraft to study them.

Long ago, some Arctic people thought northern lights were spirits playing soccer in the sky.

Scientists can predict when northern lights will appear. Information from the Sun and the solar wind in space is used.

Every display of northern lights is unique. The pattern of the lights continually shifts and changes.

"Aurora" was the name of the ancient Roman goddess of dawn.

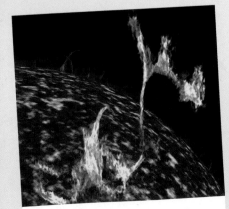

Solar flares can release up to 10 million times more energy than a volcanic eruption.

The earliest record of northern lights comes from a clay tablet more than 2,500 years old.

Some people claim they have heard sounds from northern lights.

Northern Lights
Brain Teasers

1 What is another name for northern lights?

2 What feature of the Sun causes northern lights?

3 What color is most often seen in northern lights?

4 Which type of northern lights looks like a shining curtain?

5 What glows to create northern lights?

6 What was Kristian Birkeland's **theory** about northern lights?

7 Is Earth the only planet with auroras?

8 Where do northern lights occur?

9 Which season is best for viewing northern lights?

10 How do scientists predict when there will be northern lights?

ANSWERS: 1. Aurora borealis **2.** Sunspots or solar flares **3.** Green **4.** An auroral arc **5.** Gases in the atmosphere **6.** Northern lights are caused by particles from the Sun trapped in Earth's magnetic field. **7.** No. Other planets also have them. **8.** In the auroral oval over the magnetic north pole **9.** Winter **10.** By studying the Sun and solar wind

Science in Action

See a Magnetic Field

This activity should be done with an adult.

Materials Needed

bar magnet

white card stock paper

iron filings

Directions

1 Set the card stock paper on a flat surface. Set the magnet down nearby.

2 Pour some iron filings onto the paper. Shake the paper gently from side to side to spread the filings in a thin layer.

3 Gently lift the paper and move it slowly over the magnet.

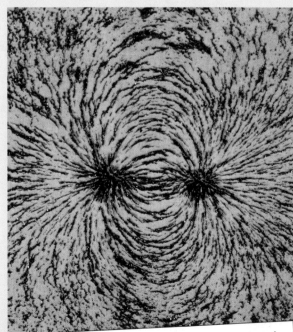

4 You should see the filings move toward the magnet in a set pattern. The pattern shows you the location of this magnetic field. This is the way Earth's magnetic field attracts particles from solar winds at its poles.

Key Words

altitudes: distance above ground

atmosphere: the body of gases that surrounds Earth

climate: the usual weather in a region throughout the year

kroner: money used in Norway

magnetic field: the area around Earth caused by attraction between the north and south poles

myths: old stories that often explain something in nature

particles: tiny bits of matter that can be solid, liquid, or gas

polar regions: the areas close to the north and south poles

solar system: the Sun and everything that orbits it

solar winds: the flow of particles away from the Sun

theory: an idea to test

thermosphere: the layer of Earth's atmosphere directly below the outermost layer

Index

Log on to www.av2books.com

AV² by Weigl brings you media enhanced books that support active learning. Go to www.av2books.com, and enter the special code found on page 2 of this book. You will gain access to enriched and enhanced content that supplements and complements this book. Content includes video, audio, weblinks, quizzes, a slide show, and activities.

Audio
Listen to sections of the book read aloud.

Video
Watch informative video clips.

Embedded Weblinks
Gain additional information for research.

Try This!
Complete activities and hands-on experiments.

WHAT'S ONLINE?

Try This!	Embedded Weblinks	Video	EXTRA FEATURES
Complete a northern lights color spectrum activity.	Learn more about the northern lights.	Watch a video about the northern lights.	**Audio** Listen to sections of the book read aloud.
Identify the types of northern lights.	Find out more about the parts of the world where the northern lights are visible.	Watch a video about solar winds.	**Key Words** Study vocabulary, and complete a matching word activity.
Try a magnetic field activity.	Read more about the science behind how auroras form.		**Slide Show** View images and captions, and prepare a presentation.
Test your knowledge of the northern lights.	Learn more about the technology used to study the northern lights.		**Quizzes** Test your knowledge.

AV² was built to bridge the gap between print and digital. We encourage you to tell us what you like and what you want to see in the future.
Sign up to be an AV² Ambassador at www.av2books.com/ambassador.